RSPCA

FRAZER SWIFT
(SERIES EDITOR: ROB ALCRAFT)

First published in Great Britain by Heinemann Library
Halley Court, Jordan Hill, Oxford OX2 8EJ
a division of Reed Educational and Professional Publishing Ltd

OXFORD FLORENCE PRAGUE MADRID ATHENS
MELBOURNE AUCKLAND KUALA LUMPUR SINGAPORE TOKYO
IBADAN NAIROBI KAMPALA JOHANNESBURG GABORONE
PORTSMOUTH NH CHICAGO MEXICO CITY SAO PAULO

Produced by Plum Creative (01590 612970)
Printed in China

01 00 99 98 97
10 9 8 7 6 5 4 3 2 1

ISBN 0 431 02757 9
This title is also available in a hardback edition (ISBN 0 431 02756 0).

British Library Cataloguing in Publication Data
        Swift, Frazer
        RSPCA. - (Taking Action)
        1. Royal Society for the Prevention of
        Cruelty to Animals - Juvenile literature
        I. Title
        361.7'632

Acknowledgements
The publishers would like to thank the following for permission to reproduce photographs:
A. Bennett p12 lower; A. Donohoe p29 middle; P. Herrmann p12 upper, p13 upper and lower, p27 upper; I. Jackson p9, p19 middle; Mr and Mrs R. Lawrence p28; LINK photography p5; A. Linscott p5 main, p7, p15 lower, p19 lower; J. Maiden p25; K. McKay p4 lower, p6 lower, p16 both, p17 both, p21 both, p24 lower; Dr C. Murphy p4 upper; J. Plant p26; A. Routh p13 middle; T. Sambrook p10, p11 all, p14 both, p15 upper, p29 upper; C. Seddon p5 inset, p6 upper, p8, p27 lower, p29 lower; South West News Service p14 upper; M. Votier p22.

Cover photograph reproduced with permission of Geoff Langan.
Cover illustration by Scott Rhodes.

Every effort has been made to contact copyright holders of any material reproduced in this book. Any omissions will be rectified in subsequent printings if notice is given to the publisher.

All words in the text appearing in bold like **this** are explained in the Glossary.

CONTENTS

WHAT'S THE PROBLEM?

Britain is known as a nation of animal lovers, but sometimes people treat animals badly. Many people feel very strongly about cruelty to animals and animal **welfare** issues are often in the news. It is a subject that causes lots of discussion and sometimes disagreement.

> **Each year nearly three million animals are used in experiments. This includes testing the safety of new products or developing new medical treatments. Experiments can cause pain, suffering and distress. Many animals kept in *laboratories* live in small, bare cages with nothing to do.**

> **Over 750 million farm animals are *reared* in the UK every year – around 14 for every person. Many are kept in cramped conditions which prevent them from moving freely.**

Traffic, *pollution* and litter can injure and kill wild animals. New roads and buildings can also destroy their homes. Some wild animals, such as foxes and deer, are hunted in ways which can be cruel.

Pets can suffer because their owners lose interest in them or because they do not know how to care for them properly. Often people decide to get a pet without realizing how much time and attention it will need, or how much it will cost to keep.

There are around seven million dogs in the UK.

WHAT DOES THE RSPCA DO?

The Royal Society for the Prevention of Cruelty to Animals (RSPCA) cares for animals that are in need of help and encourages people to be kind to animals. The Society is a **charity** and does not receive any money from the government. It depends on **donations** from the public to enable it to do its work.

COMMITTED TO CARING

The RSPCA was set up in London in 1824 and is the oldest animal **welfare** organization in the world. With a team of over 300 inspectors throughout England and Wales, it is also the largest. The Society is so big that it has been split into 10 regions throughout the country, each one with smaller 'branches' run by **volunteers**.

Lots of people know that the RSPCA helps pets, but the Society is concerned about cruelty to all animals – pets, wildlife, farm animals and animals used in **laboratories**.

▲ **Injured seals, birds caught in** *oil slicks*, **foxes hurt in traffic accidents and** *orphaned* **hedgehogs and rabbits are just some of the cases treated at RSPCA wildlife hospitals. As many animals as possible are returned to the wild when they are better.**

▶ **Sick and injured animals are treated at RSPCA clinics and hospitals. These provide a service for people who can't afford veterinary bills. Many of the patients, like this dog, are pets that have been hurt on the roads.**

RSPCA animal centres find new homes for animals whose owners are unable to look after them properly, or who treat them badly. New homes are carefully checked to make sure that the animals will be safe and have everything they need.

Each year the RSPCA's clinics and hospitals treat over 250,000 animals.

HOW DOES THE RSPCA HELP?

The RSPCA provides advice and training for animal **welfare** organizations in other countries. It also encourages scientists to find alternatives to animal experiments and asks farmers to improve conditions for their animals.

KINDER FARMING

Freedom Food, the RSPCA's animal welfare food-labelling scheme, is another way the Society is improving animals' lives. Freedom Food farms are inspected to make sure that the animals have proper living conditions and are well cared for. So shoppers buying Freedom Food meat, eggs and dairy products can be sure that the animals had a good life.

The RSPCA works with the police to take people to court who have been cruel to animals. It also persuades the government to improve the law to stop people mistreating animals.

PUTTING THE MESSAGE ACROSS

Experts at the Society's headquarters in West Sussex provide information on how to care for animals and produce magazines, videos, posters and leaflets. They let people know about the problems faced by animals by writing articles, giving interviews on radio and TV and by putting adverts in newspapers and magazines. Education staff also give talks in schools and organize animal-friendly activities for young people.

◀ **Farm animals are often transported long distances across Europe in lorries. The RSPCA's Special Operations Unit checks whether animals are given enough rest, food and water on these journeys. They also secretly investigate illegal and cruel sports like dog fighting.**

In the European Union, 270 million hens liv

Inspectors look into many different kinds of complaints about cruelty to animals. These are often about pets, but sometimes they involve farm animals and wildlife. Inspectors rescue animals in danger and give advice on caring for animals. They also monitor conditions in zoos, pet shops, *livestock markets*, race courses, kennels, catteries and *abattoirs*.

Over 32,000 people are members of the RSPCA.

MEET CARROLL LAMPORT

RSPCA INSPECTOR

I've been an RSPCA inspector for over 12 years. It's difficult to describe an inspector's job because every day is different.

Most of my time is spent responding to calls from the public. This might involve visiting a house to check on someone's pet, rescuing an injured wild animal, or making sure that farm animals are well looked after. Often it's a case of giving some common sense advice, but sometimes I have to persuade owners to give up their animals to the RSPCA so that they can be given new homes. Occasionally, as a last resort, we have to **prosecute** people.

Being an inspector is a demanding job. I still get upset when I see animals suffering or angry when people are deliberately cruel to them. But it's also the most rewarding job I can imagine.

8.00am Every morning I make sure that I have everything I might need. My van is packed with all kinds of things, from wellies and bite-proof gloves to pet food and equipment such as 'graspers', for catching dangerous dogs, badgers and foxes.

8.30am I telephone the Regional Communications Centre to find out what I'm going to be doing today. All the telephone calls about suspected animal cruelty in the area are answered here.

9.30am My first case is a dog that has been locked in a flat on its own for three or four days. I can see the dog — a Yorkshire terrier — through the letterbox and it looks very thin. So I put some dog food through the letterbox. I'll come back tomorrow to see if the owners have returned. If they haven't, then I'll have to ask the police to open the door so that I can make sure the dog is OK.

▼ **Most people are not deliberately cruel to their pets, but lack of proper care and attention can cause a great deal of suffering.**

10

Inspectors investigate around 110,000 reports of cruelty every year.

> **RSPCA inspectors often visit farms, so a pair of wellies is a crucial part of our equipment!**

10.45am The next case is just around the corner — a cat that may need help. It's obvious that the cat is very ill — she seems to have a mouth infection and is losing a lot of her fur. The owners are very elderly and I advise them to take her to the local veterinary surgeon as soon as possible. I will call back later in the week to see how they got on.

1.30pm It's a 90-kilometre drive to my third case — a cow with an injured leg. A group of walkers saw the cow in a field yesterday and reported it by calling the RSPCA's emergency number. The farmer is very concerned, but all his animals seem to be in good condition — the walkers must have been mistaken.

2.30pm A late lunch. There is also time to catch up on some paperwork before heading off to my last case — a dog that may have been mistreated.

3.30pm We get lots of calls from people who think that their neighbours are being cruel to their pets. Often, as on this occasion, it's simply a case of passing on some basic pet care advice.

No one day in my life is the same as the next—that is one of the joys of this job.

Many of my cases involve dogs, so I have to be able to handle them with confidence. Some can be difficult, but most are well-behaved and are not a problem.

Each year the RSPCA prosecutes around 1000 people.

MEET ASH BENNETT
WILDLIFE ASSISTANT

I work at the RSPCA's Stapeley Grange Wildlife Hospital in Cheshire. Animals are brought here by RSPCA inspectors and members of the public. We treat thousands of sick and injured wild animals every year.

Being a wildlife assistant isn't a nine-to-five job. Sick animals need attention around the clock – so I often have to work at weekends and through the night.

My job is to feed the animals, clean out their pens, check on their progress and let the hospital veterinary surgeon know how they are doing. But by far the best part of my job is releasing the animals back into the wild when they have recovered.

8.00am The first thing I do when I arrive at the hospital is check all the animals and give them their morning medicine. If there are any problems, for example if they're not eating, I tell the veterinary surgeon and write the details on the animals' record cards.

9.30am Feeding time. Preparing the food is an important job because it needs to be just right if the animals are to make a speedy recovery. Many of the **orphaned mammals** and **nestlings** have to be hand-fed. This can be a problem because we want animals to remain as wild as possible, and getting too used to humans makes it difficult for them to adapt to life back in the wild.

▲ **We care for lots of *orphaned* animals, like this badger cub, who are too young to look after themselves.**

11.00am I take a close look at a young fox that had an operation yesterday. She was brought to the hospital by an RSPCA ambulance driver after being hit by a car. She was very ill, but with lots of rest it shouldn't be too long before she can be returned to the wild.

▲ **Swans can be difficult to handle, so I try to get one of the other wildlife assistants to help me.**

▲ **We see lots of foxes and badgers that have been injured on roads.**

12.00pm I'm called to the hospital reception to have a look at a hedgehog that has been brought in by a member of the public. A quick examination reveals that it has an injured leg. I take the details of where and when the hedgehog was found and let the veterinary surgeon know that it needs attention.

1.00pm I give the swans their injections. Most of the swans we get at the hospital are ill because they have eaten lead fishing weights or shotgun pellets. It can take several weeks for them to recover fully.

2.30pm Time to clean out the pens — not my favourite job, but it has to be done!

4.30pm I go to the **aviary** to feed the owls. Most owls are **nocturnal**, so we don't feed them until the end of the day. I always make a note of how much food they have eaten and keep an eye on their progress, for example to check whether they can fly or not.

◀ **This little owl was admitted to the hospital with a broken wing.**

13

There are around 1.5 million hedgehogs in Great Britain

MEET JACQUELINE GLIDE
REHOMING VISITOR

I'm a **volunteer** and I work at an RSPCA animal centre in Surrey. I find new homes for unwanted, **stray** or abandoned animals. Most of the animals are dogs and cats, but we also get lots of smaller pets such as rabbits, guinea pigs and even ferrets!

Too many people get a pet without realizing how much attention it will need, or how much it will cost to keep. Another problem is that lots of people find puppies and kittens irresistible, but lose interest in them when they grow up and become less cute. Then there are all the unwanted **litters** that would be so easy to avoid if more people had their pets **neutered**.

My job is to check out people who want to **adopt** an animal. I find out why they want an animal and whether they realize how having a pet will change their lives. I visit their homes to see if their houses and gardens are suitable. If they already have pets, I also make sure that these are properly cared for.

10.00am The first of two home visits this morning — a family who would like to adopt a cat. A home away from busy roads is particularly important for a cat. It's also vital that the family doesn't have any pets that would be at risk from a cat, such as budgerigars or mice! After a long chat, I report back to the animal centre manager who decides the family will make ideal adopters.

▲ **Meeting people face-to-face is an essential part of my job. I have to be sure that they will be able to provide the animals with a safe and happy home.**

11.30am I head off to meet a couple who would like a dog. As soon as I arrive I realize that a big dog would not be a good pet for them — their house is tiny! It's possible to find out a lot about people on the telephone, but it's only by visiting them that you can be really sure of what type of pet would be suitable.

Every year the RSPCA finds new homes for over 80,000 animals.

1.00pm Back at the animal centre. I like to be here on Saturday afternoons because this is our busiest time, with lots of people dropping in to find out about adopting a pet. Often they don't realize that they have to be approved before we can let them have an animal, so I like to be on hand to explain why the **welfare** of the animal has to come first.

3.00pm A woman arrives at the reception desk and says she is interested in adopting two puppies. This is good news because we have quite a few puppies at the moment. It's not long before she finds the ones she would like — two sisters from the same litter. I arrange to visit her home tomorrow.

Cats need lots of care and attention. They can live for more than 16 years. Having a cat as a pet is a life-long commitment.

Dogs at the animal centre are usually very excited when visitors stop to say hello.

5.00pm I stop off on the way home to check on the progress of Tin Tin, a lovely cat that was adopted last week. I was a little worried about him because he's a very nervous cat, but he seems to have settled down very well in his new home. Another happy ending!

There are around 500,000 stray dogs in the UK.

MEET BAIRBRE O'MALLEY
VETERINARY SURGEON

I'm a veterinary surgeon at the RSPCA's busy Harmsworth Memorial Hospital in north London. Most of our patients are pets, but it's not unusual for people to bring along sick or injured wild animals that they've found. So I've got to be prepared for everything!

Most animals are brought in by their owners because they are ill or need a routine operation. Some cases are simple – dogs that need their claws clipped, or cats with flea problems. Others are more complicated, such as animals injured in road traffic accidents or animals with serious diseases such as cancer. We also treat **stray** animals that are found wandering the streets by RSPCA inspectors or the police.

Being a veterinary surgeon is a very rewarding job. It's great to know that you've saved animals' lives. But seeing animals in pain can be distressing. The worst thing is putting animals to sleep – that's never easy.

8.30am Every morning starts with a check on the overnight progress of all the patients. The hospital is full this morning. With 100 animals to see, ward rounds can take a long time!

10.30am My first road traffic accident victim of the day – a dog called Ben who was hit by a car earlier this morning. The first thing to do is to examine him to see how much damage has been done. An X-ray may be needed later if we suspect serious injuries. Road traffic accidents – we call them RTAs – are one of the biggest causes of serious injuries to cats and dogs. This one looks like he might be lucky – just a few cuts and bruises.

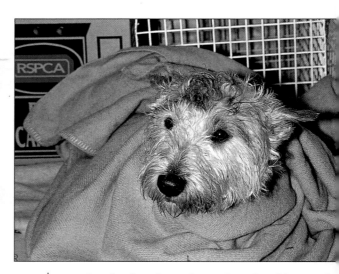

▲ **Animals that have been involved in road traffic accidents are often in a state of shock when they arrive at the hospital.**

People have been keeping dogs as pets for over 10,000 years.

12.00am Down to the operating theatre. We carry out about 20 operations every day. This one is to remove a lump from a dog's leg. He'll be up and about in no time!

2.00pm After a quick lunch it's afternoon surgery. The waiting room is bursting at the seams. This is my favourite part of the job because I like meeting lots of people and I never know what to expect. My first case is a cat called Ruby with a really bad tummy problem. I'm not sure what the cause of the problem is so I decide to admit her to the hospital so that we can carry out a few tests.

▼ Veterinary nurses are an important part of the team at Harmsworth Hospital.

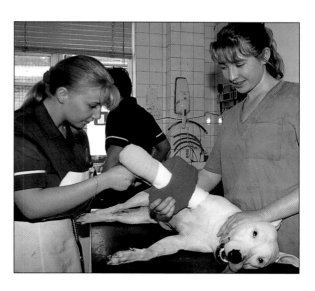

▼ Many animals need a thorough examination in order to find out what they are suffering from. An extra pair of hands is very useful!

5.30pm It's been a long day — we've seen over 180 animals. But before I go home I look in on Ben, the little dog I saw this morning. He's doing really well — perhaps he could go home tomorrow.

Cats are the most popular pet in the UK.

WORK IN EDUCATION

The RSPCA has a team of over 40 education and school liaison officers around England and Wales who visit schools and colleges. They encourage people to be kind to animals by explaining the problems that they face and by giving advice on how to care for them.

SPREADING THE WORD

The Society produces booklets, posters and videos for schools and provides training courses for teachers. It encourages all schools to become more animal-friendly by setting up wildlife gardens in their grounds. These allow pupils to learn from observing animals in their natural **habitats**, rather than by keeping them in the classroom.

ACTION FOR ANIMALS

The RSPCA also runs the Animal Action Club – the RSPCA's club for under 17s – and organizes competitions, fun award schemes and Animal Adventure activity days. Mallydams Wood, the RSPCA's study centre near Hastings in East Sussex, runs animal **welfare** courses in subjects such as caring for pets and **first aid** for injured wildlife.

▲ Education has always been a vital part of the RSPCA's work. Helping young people to be kind to animals is the best way of making sure that animals do not suffer in the future.

◀ **RSPCA Animal Adventures give young people a chance to meet new friends and to find out about all kinds of animals and the problems they face. Activities include visits to woodlands, RSPCA hospitals, farms and the seashore.**

▶ **Litter can be a big problem for animals. They can get trapped in tins, cut themselves on glass or become ill if they mistake rubbish for food. School liaison officers help pupils realize that dropping litter is bad for animals and the environment.**

◀ **Education is important at the Society's three wildlife hospitals. Each one has an education centre where schools and other groups of young people can go to find out about the problems faced by wild animals.**

Over 20,000 young people are members of the Animal Action Club.

WORK IN THE MEDIA

The media – TV, radio, newspapers and magazines – is the main way the RSPCA lets people know about its work. This is also a very useful way of giving people information about animal **welfare** issues in the news.

ON THE CAMPAIGN TRAIL

Some animal welfare issues are controversial– they cause disagreement or argument. **Fox-hunting** is a good example. The RSPCA thinks that fox-hunting is cruel, but fox-hunters and some farmers say that it is a good way of controlling fox numbers.

IN THE NEWS

Animal experiments are another controversial subject that many people feel strongly about. By giving interviews on radio and TV, writing articles for magazines and giving newspapers information in press releases, the RSPCA provides the facts so that people can make up their own minds about issues like these.

➤ **The RSPCA produces two of its own magazines – one for adults called** *Animal Life* **and one for young people called** *Animal Action* **– as well as over 200 different leaflets and posters.**

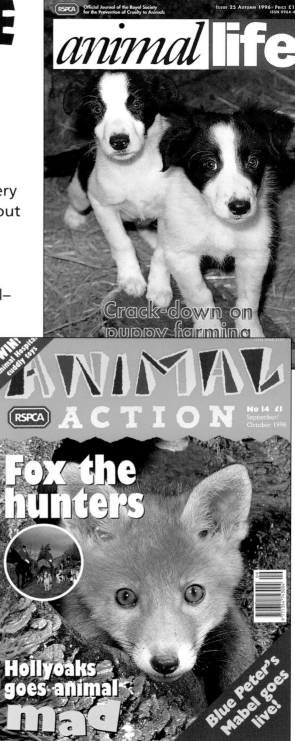

Around 20,000 foxes are killed in hunts every year.

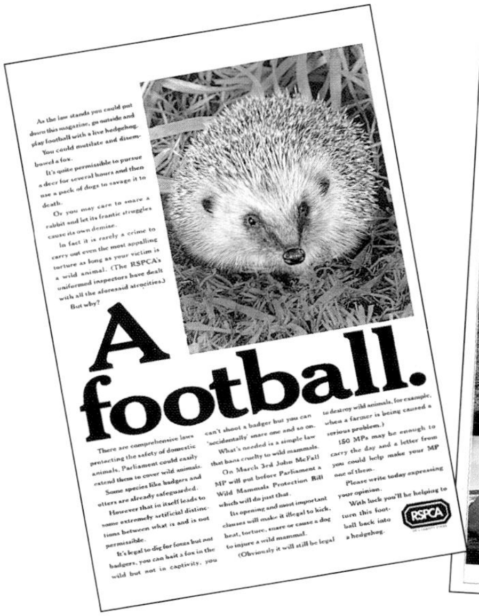
As the law stands you could put down this magazine, go outside and play football with a live hedgehog.
You could mutilate and disembowel a fox.
It's quite permissible to pursue a deer for several hours and then use a pack of dogs to savage it to death.
Or you may care to snare a rabbit and let its frantic struggles cause its own demise.
In fact it is rarely a crime to carry out even the most appalling torture as long as your victim is a wild animal. (The RSPCA's uniformed inspectors have dealt with all the aforesaid atrocities.)
But why?
A football.
There are comprehensive laws protecting the safety of domestic animals. Parliament could easily extend them to cover wild animals.
Some species like badgers and otters are already safeguarded.
However that in itself leads to some extremely artificial distinctions between what is and is not permissible.
It's legal to dig for foxes but not badgers, you can bait a fox in the wild but not in captivity, you can't shoot a badger but you can 'accidentally' snare one and so on.
What's needed is a simple law that bans cruelty to wild mammals.
On March 3rd John McFall MP will put before Parliament a Wild Mammals Protection Bill which will do just that.
Its opening and most important clauses will make it illegal to kick, beat, torture, snare or cause a dog to injure a wild mammal.
(Obviously it will still be legal to destroy wild animals, for example, when a farmer is being caused a serious problem.)
150 MPs may be enough to carry the day and a letter from you could help make your MP one of them.
Please write today expressing your opinion.
With luck you'll be helping to turn this football back into a hedgehog.
RSPCA

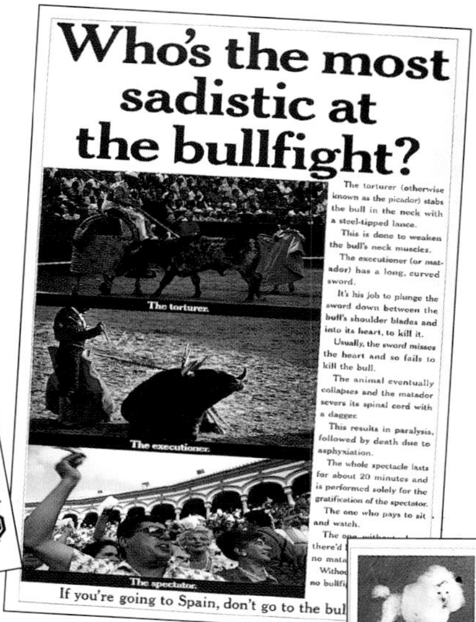
Who's the most sadistic at the bullfight?
The torturer.
The executioner.
The spectator.
The torturer (otherwise known as the picador) stabs the bull in the neck with a steel-tipped lance.
This is done to weaken the bull's neck muscles.
The executioner (or matador) has a long, curved sword.
It's his job to plunge the sword down between the bull's shoulder blades and into its heart, to kill it.
Usually, the sword misses the heart and so fails to kill the bull.
The animal eventually collapses and the matador severs its spinal cord with a dagger.
This results in paralysis, followed by death due to asphyxiation.
The whole spectacle lasts for about 20 minutes and is performed solely for the gratification of the spectator.
The one who pays to sit and watch.
If you're going to Spain, don't go to the bul

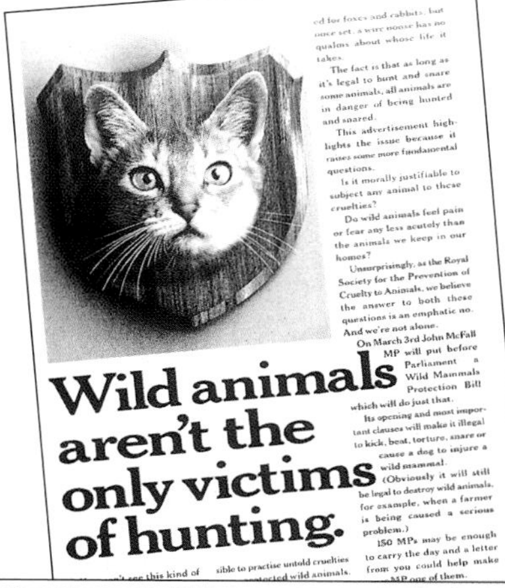
ed for foxes and rabbits, but once set, a wire noose has no qualms about whose life it takes.
The fact is that as long as it's legal to hunt and snare some animals, all animals are in danger of being hunted and snared.
This advertisement highlights the issue because it raises some more fundamental questions.
Is it morally justifiable to subject any animal to these cruelties?
Do wild animals feel pain or fear any less acutely than the animals we keep in our homes?
Unsurprisingly, as the Royal Society for the Prevention of Cruelty to Animals, we believe the answer to both these questions is an emphatic no.
And we're not alone.
On March 3rd John McFall MP will put before Parliament a Wild Mammals Protection Bill which will do just that.
Its opening and most important clauses will make it illegal to kick, beat, torture, snare or cause a dog to injure a wild mammal.
(Obviously it will still be legal to destroy wild animals, for example, when a farmer is being caused a serious problem.)
150 MPs may be enough to carry the day and a letter from you could help make
Wild animals aren't the only victims of hunting.

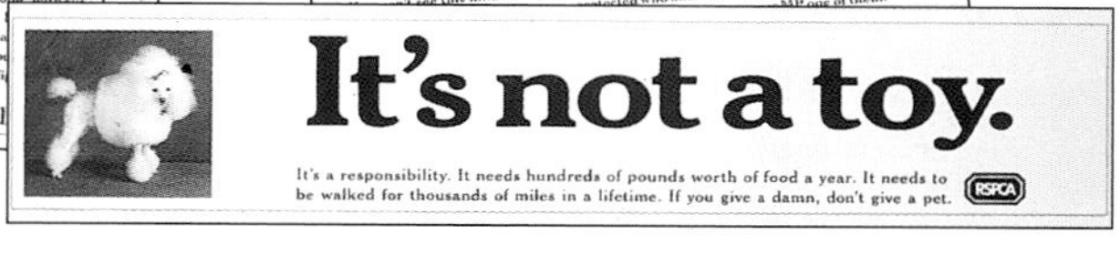
It's not a toy.
It's a responsibility. It needs hundreds of pounds worth of food a year. It needs to be walked for thousands of miles in a lifetime. If you give a damn, don't give a pet.
RSPCA

The RSPCA puts adverts in newspapers and magazines to let people know about animal welfare problems and to get support for its point of view. This is called campaigning.

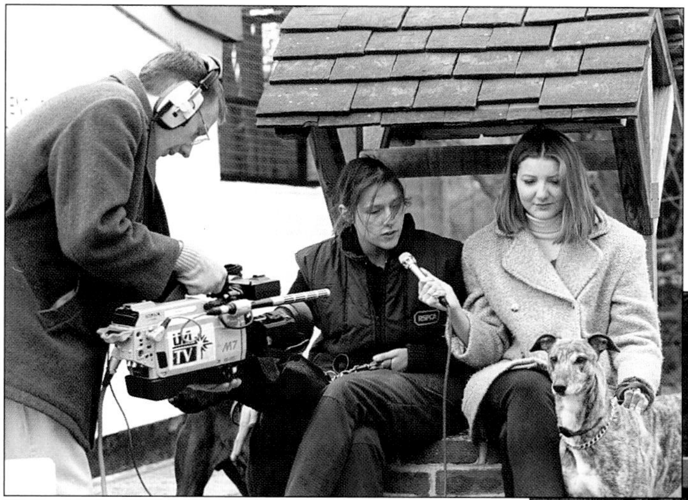
RSPCA

RSPCA experts often appear on TV and radio news programmes. They are also regularly interviewed by reporters from national and regional newspapers.

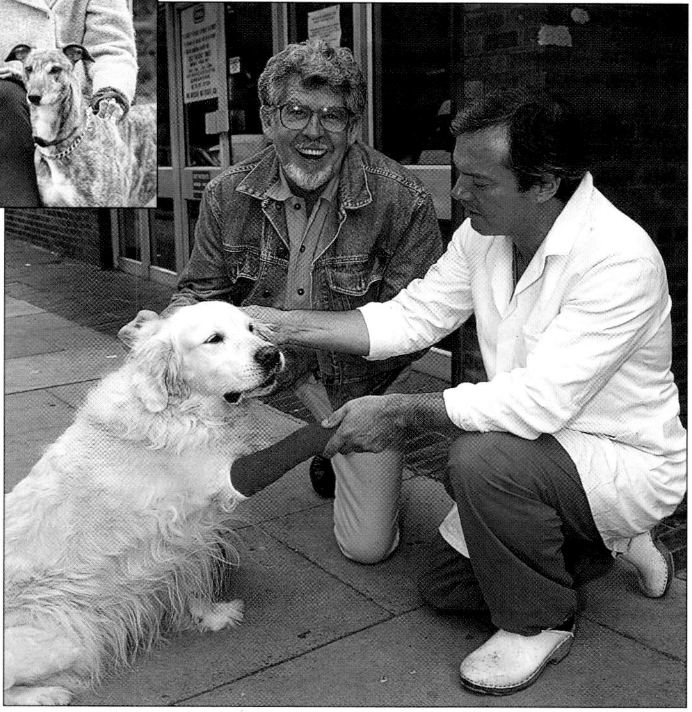

One of the BBC's most popular television programmes, *Animal Hospital*, was based at the RSPCA's Harmsworth Hospital in north London. Here is the hospital's veterinary director David Grant with presenter Rolf Harris and another satisfied customer!

Each year over two million animals are used in experiments.

WORK IN OTHER COUNTRIES

Cruelty to animals is a problem all over the world. In some countries animals are treated very badly, often because people do not know how to care for them. Sometimes the cruelty is deliberate. For example, many people think that **bullfighting** is cruel, but it is a popular sport in Spain, Portugal, France and South America.

WELFARE WORLDWIDE

A very important part of the RSPCA's work is to help animal **welfare** organizations in other countries.

Sometimes this means giving them money for new buildings or to buy new equipment and medicines. But the most important help is in the form of expert advice and training. The Society also works to persuade foreign governments to change laws to give animals more protection from cruelty.

▼ **Holiday-makers from the UK are often shocked by conditions in some foreign zoos. Many animals are kept in cages that are too small and prevent them from doing many of the things they would do in the wild.**

The RSPCA works with 400 animal welfare organizations around the world.

▲ Animal circuses are unpopular in Britain, but abroad many circuses still train animals to perform tricks. Animals are often kept in poor conditions when they are not performing. Travelling from town to town can also be stressful for the animals.

▶ This boy cares for his dog, but in some countries people do not look after their animals. Perhaps they don't have enough money to feed their pets properly or to pay veterinary bills. There are also lots of *stray* and unwanted animals because people can't afford to have their pets *neutered*.

Around 10,000 bulls are killed in bullfights in Spain every year.

WORK IN THE COMMUNITY

Many of the RSPCA's animal clinics and rehoming centres are paid for by local branches and mainly staffed by volunteers.

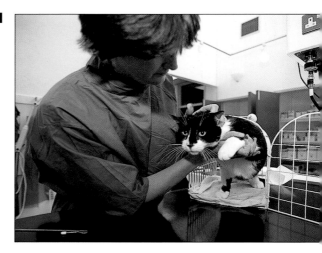

The RSPCA plays a vital role in the local community by providing people who cannot afford veterinary bills with low-cost veterinary treatment for their pets. It also helps cut down the number of **stray** cats and dogs by **neutering** and **microchipping** animals at a price their owners can afford.

PEOPLE POWER

Like many **charities**, the RSPCA depends on thousands of **volunteers** to do much of its work. Volunteers are not paid for their work, but give up their free time to help the Society care for animals. All kinds of people volunteer, but they all have one thing in common – a love of animals.

Volunteers run the RSPCA's 200 branches and provide a valuable service to local communities. The RSPCA runs shops that sell clothes, toys, books and other goods that are donated by the public. All are staffed mainly by volunteers.

Volunteers exercise dogs for people who are too old or ill to walk them themselves. They also look after unwanted animals until new owners can be found.

24

A dog costs around £700 a year to keep.

LOCAL SUPPORT

Probably the most important job volunteers do is to raise money for the Society. This is known as fund-raising. They do this in lots of ways – by collecting money in shopping centres, holding jumble sales and by organizing sponsored swims and walks.

Branches play an important part in organizing RSPCA Week, an annual event which draws attention to the work of the RSPCA as well as raising funds. All the money is spent on helping animals in the local area.

 Actress Letitia Dean joins members of the RSPCA's Lincoln Branch, at the opening of their new animal centre.

Only 15–20% of dogs and cats are neutered.

THE MILFORD HAVEN OIL SPILL

Imagine an **oil slick** 48 km long. Now think about the damage it could do to the animals that live or feed in the sea.

The tanker *Sea Empress* **ran aground** as it entered Milford Haven harbour on the night of 15 February 1996. During the following week over 75,000 tonnes of oil were spilled into the sea.

This part of the Welsh coastline is one of the most important wildlife **habitats** in Europe. Hundreds of thousands of sea birds, seals and other animals were at risk from the oil.

CLOGGED FEATHERS

Oil ruins the natural **insulation** and waterproofing of birds' feathers. Feathers keep birds warm and enable them to float in water by trapping air.

Oil pollution at sea and in rivers is a big problem for animals.

It costs around £30 to clean each oiled bird.

Oil prevents feathers from doing their job, so the birds can get very cold and cannot float. They can die of **hypothermia** if they are not rescued and cleaned. Birds covered in oil are unable to fly because their feathers stick together. Another danger is that oil can be poisonous if animals eat it while trying to clean themselves.

DEALING WITH DISASTER

The RSPCA is always prepared for this kind of disaster and is able to respond very quickly. Oil **pollution** is a constant threat around Britain's coast, but thankfully most oil spills are not as serious as this one. A rescue operation was immediately started to save as many birds and other animals as possible. At the same time the RSPCA set up a disaster **appeal** so that people could give money towards the operation.

RSPCA inspectors from all over England and Wales arrived at Milford Haven to organize teams of **volunteers** on the beaches. Their job was to collect the birds that had been affected and to take them to an RSPCA **first aid** centre that had been set up in a nearby warehouse. Hundreds of birds were also taken to RSPCA wildlife hospitals in Cheshire, Norfolk and Somerset for specialist treatment and cleaning. Many birds died before they could be helped, but over 1400 birds were saved, including herring gulls, oystercatchers, guillemots, scoters and swans.

Staff at the RSPCA's wildlife hospitals are experts at cleaning birds that have been caught in oil. The birds are thoroughly washed with *detergent* and lots of hot water until all the oil has been removed.

When the birds are fully recovered they are returned to the wild.

Every year there are hundreds of oil spills around Britain's coast.

VISION FOR THE FUTURE

Animals are a very important part of our lives. They keep us company and provide us with food and clothing. Some animals, like police horses, sheep dogs and guide dogs help us do our jobs or get around safely. Some people use animals in sports, such as horse- and dog-racing. Scientists use animals to develop medicines and treatments and to test the safety of everyday products. Life would be very different without animals.

Despite the hard work of the RSPCA and other animal **welfare** organizations, more and more animals are suffering. The RSPCA's vision for the future is a world where all animals have everything they need to be happy and healthy. Animal welfare organizations would not be needed because everyone would know how to treat animals and their **habitats** properly.

The RSPCA would like to see a future where people all over the world treat animals with the kindness they deserve.

▶ **The RSPCA believes that too many animals suffer in too many experiments. Reducing the number of animals used and improving conditions are immediate priorities.**

Six out of every ten households in the UK have a pet.

The RSPCA believes that people should only get a pet if they are sure they can give it everything it needs to be happy and healthy.

The RSPCA believes that farm animals should have a decent life and be kept in conditions which allow them to move freely.

The RSPCA believes that wild animals and their habitats should be treated with respect.

Over 750 million farm animals are reared in the UK every year.

WHAT YOU CAN DO TO HELP

If you would like to help animals have a better life there are lots of things you could do.

- Always treat animals with kindness.

- Try not to disturb animals' homes.

- Think very carefully before you get a pet. Owning any kind of pet, no matter how big or small, is a big responsibility. Find out about the animal before you decide – your library will have plenty of books on pets. Your local veterinary surgeon may also be able to give you some advice. Make sure you can give the animal everything it needs to be happy and healthy.

- Never drop litter and **recycle** as much rubbish as possible.

- Look out for animal-friendly products and remember to read labels carefully.

- Write to the RSPCA if you would like information about caring for animals.

- If you see an animal in need of help do not touch it. Let an adult know and ask them to call the RSPCA emergency line on 0990 555999.

If you would like more information about the work of the RSPCA or would like to join the Animal Action Club, please contact:

RSPCA,
Causeway,
Horsham,
West Sussex RH12 1HG.
Tel: 01403 264181

GLOSSARY

abattoirs places where farm animals are killed, also called slaughterhouses.

adopt to take responsibility for and look after a child or animal

appeal a public request for money to raise funds to deal with a problem or emergency

aviary an enclosure where birds are kept

bullfighting a traditional sport where bulls are killed for entertainment

charity a non-profit-making organization set up to help those in need

detergent a substance used with water to clean away dirt

donations gifts of money or goods given by people out of kindness

first aid help given to an injured person or animal until full medical treatment can be provided

fox-hunting an activity where foxes are chased and killed by people on horseback and a pack of dogs.

habitat an animal's or plant's natural home, such as a forest, lake or hedgerow

hypothermia a dangerous medical condition where the temperature of the body is very low

insulation a layer that helps stop heat escaping, such as an animal's fur or feathers

laboratories places where research and scientific experiments are carried out

litter group name for all the young animals produced by a mother in one birth

livestock markets places where farm animals are bought and sold

mammals warm-blooded animals with backbones. Mammals have fur and give birth to live young, which feed on their mother's milk.

microchipping a way of giving animals an electronic name tag to help owners find lost pets. A tiny electronic chip, the size of a grain of rice, is painlessly put under the animal's skin. This can then be scanned to find out the animal's name, address and medical records.

nestling a young bird totally dependent on being fed and cared for by its parents

neutered a neutered animal has had an operation to stop it breeding (having young)

nocturnal active at night

oil slick a patch of oil on the surface of areas of water such as the sea or rivers

orphaned young people or animals whose parents are dead

pollution damage to the natural world

prosecute to take someone to court who is accused of doing something against the law

reared to have brought up and looked after an animal until it is able to look after itself

recycle to use materials again.

run aground ships and boats run aground when they enter water that is too shallow. The ship's bottom drags along the bed of the sea or river until it becomes stuck.

stray animals that wander away from their homes and become lost

volunteers people who work without being paid

welfare the health and happiness, or well-being, of an animal or person

INDEX